Bossing Investments: A Smart Girl's Guide to Building Wealth

Bossing Up

Sophie Johnson

Published by All-Star Scripts, 2023.

BOSSING INVESTMENTS: A SMART GIRL'S GUIDE TO BUILDING WEALTH

First edition. February 17, 2023.

ISBN: 979-8215651537

Written by Sophie Johnson.

Table of Contents

Introduction: Why You Need to Boss Your Investments

Girlies, it's time to get bossy with your investments!

Let's be real, money can be a touchy subject. It's not uncommon to feel overwhelmed and intimidated by the thought of managing your finances, especially when it comes to investing. But here's the deal, building wealth is not just for the old, rich guys on Wall Street - it's for us too, the young and ambitious girlfriends who want to secure a financially independent future.

As a young woman, I understand the pressure of feeling like we have to have it all figured out by a certain age. It's like we're in a race to have the perfect life, with the perfect job, the perfect relationship, and the perfect bank account. But here's the tea: there's no set timeline for when you should start investing or building wealth. Start where you are, use what you have, and do what you can.

I'm here to help guide you through the world of investing, so you can build the life you've always dreamed of. This book is for the girl who wants to take control of her finances, to become the main character of her financial story. It's for the girl who wants to glow up and build a life of financial freedom.

Let's be clear, being a boss at investing isn't about being extra or flashy. It's about being woke to the possibilities and the opportunities out there. It's about being smart with your money, so you can achieve your dreams and live the life you want.

Now, I'm not a financial advisor or a CEO of a big corporation. I'm just a regular girl who has been in your shoes, trying to figure out how to build wealth and financial stability. Through trial and error, research, and learning from others, I've learned how to make my money work for me. And I want to share those lessons with you.

So, if you're ready to take control of your financial future, to low-key become a boss at investing, then this book is for you. We're going to cover everything from stocks and bonds to real estate and retirement plans. It's going to be informative, fun, and maybe even a little bit sassy.

Let's do this, sis. Let's slay our investments and build the life we want. It's time to boss up and become the CEO of our financial futures. Are you with me? Let's go!

Chapter 1: The Basics of Building Wealth: How to Start Investing

I know what you might be thinking, "Investing? That's only for rich people." But sis, let me tell you, investing is for anyone who wants to build a secure financial future. It doesn't matter if you're a broke college student or a high-key successful businesswoman. If you want to be woke and take control of your money, investing is the way to go.

But before we get into the nitty-gritty of investing, let's talk about why it's so important to build wealth in the first place. Money might not buy happiness, but it sure can buy freedom. Imagine not having to stress about bills or living paycheck to paycheck. Imagine being able to travel the world or start your dream business. That's what building wealth can do for you, girlfriend.

Now, I know that investing can seem intimidating. There's all this jargon and fancy lingo that seems like it's only meant for the Wall Street elite. But don't worry, we're going to break it down for you in a way that's easy to understand. You don't have to be extra smart or have a degree in finance to start investing. All you need is a willingness to learn and a desire to build your wealth.

So, if you're ready to take on the role of the main character in your financial story, then let's get started. This chapter is all about the basics of building wealth, and we're going to cover everything from budgeting to saving to investing. Trust me, by the end of this book, you'll be a pro at building your financial empire. Let's go, girlfriends! This chapter *slaps* and we're just getting started.

BOSSING INVESTMENTS: A SMART GIRL'S GUIDE TO BUILDING WEALTH

Alright, girlfriend, **let's get down to business.** If you want to boss your investments and build wealth, you need to start investing. I know it can be intimidating, but trust me, you've got this.

First things first, let's talk about what investing is. Simply put, investing is using your money to buy assets with the expectation of making a profit. The most common types of assets people invest in are stocks, bonds, and real estate.

Now, I know what you might be thinking: "I don't have enough money to start investing!" But here's the thing: you don't need a ton of money to start investing. In fact, you can start with as little as $5 or $10 a month. The important thing is that you start.

One of the easiest ways to start investing is through a retirement account, like a 401(k) or an IRA. These accounts allow you to invest your money and save for your future retirement. And the best part? Many employers offer a 401(k) as part of their benefits package, so you don't even have to set it up yourself.

If you don't have access to a retirement account through your employer, or if you want to invest outside of a retirement account, there are plenty of other options available. One popular option is to open a brokerage account, which allows you to buy and sell stocks, bonds, and other investments.

But before you start investing, there are a few things you need to know. First and foremost, investing always carries some level of risk. No investment is completely safe or guaranteed to make you money. That's why it's important to do your research and understand the risks involved with any investment you make.

Secondly, investing is a long-term game. You're not going to get rich overnight by investing in the stock market. In fact, you're likely to experience some ups and downs along the way. But over time, history has shown that the stock market has consistently provided good returns for investors who are patient and stick to their long-term plan.

Finally, it's important to diversify your investments. This means investing in a variety of different assets, rather than putting all your money in one stock or bond. Diversification can help reduce your risk and increase your chances of long-term success.

So, to sum it up: investing is using your money to buy assets with the expectation of making a profit. You can start investing with as little as $5 or $10 a month, and there are plenty of options available, including retirement accounts and brokerage accounts. Investing always carries some level of risk, so it's important to do your research and understand the risks involved. Investing is a long-term game, and it's important to stick to your plan and be patient. And finally, diversification is key to reducing your risk and increasing your chances of success.

BOSSING INVESTMENTS: A SMART GIRL'S GUIDE TO BUILDING WEALTH

And there you have it, my beautiful friends. We've covered the basics of building wealth and how to start investing like a boss. Remember, building wealth is a journey, and it's not something that happens overnight. It takes patience, discipline, and a willingness to learn.

But the good news is that you don't have to do it alone. There are plenty of resources out there to help you along the way, from financial advisors to online courses to good old-fashioned books like this one. So keep learning, keep growing, and keep building that financial empire.

And always remember, you are capable of achieving anything you set your mind to. You are a badass at making money, and you have the power to create the financial future of your dreams. So go out there and slay, girlfriends!

Chapter 2: Understanding Your Relationship with Money: Identifying Your Money Mindset

Girlies, we all want to be financially independent, don't we? We want to be the CEO of our lives and make our dreams come true. But, the journey to financial freedom can be tough. We have bills to pay, student loans to tackle, and let's not forget our love for online shopping. But, before we start budgeting and investing, we need to understand our relationship with money. We need to identify our *money mindset*, which is the key to unlocking our financial potential. So, grab your latte, get cozy, and let's dive into Chapter 2 of our financial *glow up* journey.

Alright, girl, we're about to **get real**. Before we can start building wealth and investing, we need to take a look at our relationship with money. Your money mindset can have a big impact on your ability to achieve financial success.

First, let's talk about what a money mindset is. Simply put, your money mindset is the way you think and feel about money. It's your attitudes, beliefs, and values when it comes to money.

So, take a minute to reflect on your own money mindset. Do you feel like you're always struggling to make ends meet? Do you worry about money constantly? Do you feel like you'll never be able to get ahead financially? Or do you feel confident and in control of your finances? Do you see money as a tool to achieve your goals and build the life you want?

Your money mindset is shaped by a variety of factors, including your upbringing, your cultural background, your experiences with money, and the messages you've received about money throughout your life. And it's not always easy to change your mindset, especially if you've held certain beliefs about money for a long time.

But the good news is that it's possible to shift your money mindset and adopt new, more positive beliefs about money. Here are a few tips to get you started:

1. **Identify your limiting beliefs.** Take some time to reflect on the negative beliefs you hold about money. Do you believe that money is evil or that rich people are greedy? Do you believe that you'll never be able to achieve financial success? Once you've identified your limiting beliefs, you can start to challenge them and adopt new, more positive beliefs.

2. **Practice gratitude.** One way to shift your mindset is to focus on the positive aspects of your life and finances. Take some time each day to reflect on the things you're grateful for, including your financial resources.

3. **Surround yourself with positive influences.** Seek out people who have a positive attitude towards money and who are achieving financial success. This can help you adopt a more positive money mindset and provide inspiration for your own financial goals.

4. **Set clear financial goals.** Having clear goals for your finances can help you stay focused and motivated. Identify what you want to achieve with your money, whether it's saving for a down payment on a house or investing for your future retirement.

5. **Take action.** Ultimately, the best way to shift your money mindset is to take action towards your financial goals. As you start to see progress, you'll start to feel more confident and in control of your finances.

So, to sum it up: your money mindset is the way you think and feel about money, and it can have a big impact on your financial success. To shift your mindset and adopt a more positive attitude towards money, identify your limiting beliefs, practice gratitude, surround yourself with positive influences, set clear financial goals, and take action.

Girlfriends, we did it! We've learned so much about our money mindset and how it shapes our financial habits. We've identified our limiting beliefs and turned them into empowering affirmations. We've also learned how to prioritize our spending and invest in our financial future. Remember, being financially independent doesn't mean we have to sacrifice our joy and happiness. It means we have the power to live our best lives without financial stress. So, let's continue to work on our money mindset and *slay* our financial goals. We got this, sis!

Chapter 3: Setting Financial Goals: Defining Your Vision for the Future

Girlies, it's time to talk about the M-word: money. Yeah, we know it's not the most glamorous topic, but trust us, it's important. In fact, it's one of the most important things you can focus on if you want to achieve your dreams and live your best life.

Here's the deal: too many of us are living paycheck to paycheck, drowning in debt, and feeling totally overwhelmed when it comes to our finances. It's time to *wake up* and take control. You deserve financial independence, and it all starts with setting goals and defining your vision for the future.

Now, we know that sounds like a lot of work. But don't worry, girl, we've got your back. In this chapter, we're going to break down the steps you need to take to set your financial goals and *slay* them like the CEO you are. We're going to help you get *extra* with your money and build the kind of life you've always dreamed of.

But first, let's get real. What does financial independence even mean to you? Is it about having enough money to travel the world? Buying a house? Supporting your family? Finally being able to afford those designer shoes you've had your eye on? There's no right or wrong answer here, sis. Your vision for the future is personal to you, and it's important to get clear on what you want to achieve.

In this chapter, we'll guide you through the process of defining your vision for the future, setting specific financial goals, and figuring out how to get there. We'll share personal stories and anecdotes to illustrate key concepts, and we'll help you *glow up* your finances in a way that feels authentic to you.

So get ready, girlfriends, because we're about to take you on a journey to financial independence. It's time to become the *main character* of your own life and take control of your money. High-key, it's going to be amazing. Let's do this!

BOSSING INVESTMENTS: A SMART GIRL'S GUIDE TO BUILDING WEALTH

Why is goal setting so important? Because without clear goals, it's easy to lose focus and get off track. Setting goals helps us stay motivated and provides a roadmap for our financial journey.

So, let's talk about *how to set financial goals.* Here are some steps you can take:

1. **Define your vision.** What do you want your financial future to look like? Do you want to be debt-free? Do you want to be able to retire early? Do you want to start your own business? Visualize what you want to achieve and write it down.

2. **Set specific, measurable goals.** Once you have a vision for your financial future, it's time to set specific, measurable goals that will help you achieve that vision. For example, if you want to be debt-free, you might set a goal to pay off all of your credit card debt within the next year.

3. **Break down your goals into actionable steps.** Once you've set your goals, break them down into actionable steps that you can take. For example, if your goal is to save $10,000 for a down payment on a house, you might break that down into a monthly savings goal and identify ways to cut back on expenses in order to save more.

4. **Prioritize your goals.** If you have multiple financial goals, it's important to prioritize them. Identify which goals are most important to you and focus on those first.

5. **Track your progress.** In order to stay motivated and on track, it's important to track your progress towards your goals. Use a spreadsheet or a budgeting app to track your income, expenses, and savings. And celebrate your successes along the way!

Remember, your financial goals should be specific, measurable, and achievable. Don't be afraid to dream big, but make sure your goals are also realistic.

And one more thing: don't be afraid to adjust your goals as needed. Life is unpredictable, and your financial situation might change over time. It's okay to reassess your goals and adjust them as needed.

So, to sum it up: setting clear financial goals is essential to achieving financial success. To set your financial goals, define your vision, set specific and measurable goals, break down your goals into actionable steps, prioritize your goals, and track your progress.

BOSSING INVESTMENTS: A SMART GIRL'S GUIDE TO BUILDING WEALTH

Alright girlies, we did it! We tackled the tough topic of money and set our financial goals like the bosses we are. By defining our vision for the future, we've taken the first step towards achieving financial independence and living our best lives.

Remember, this journey is all about you. It's about figuring out what you want, setting a plan, and taking action. And trust us, there's nothing more *woke* than taking control of your finances and building a life that you love.

We hope this chapter has inspired you to take action and chase your dreams. Keep the *slaps* coming by setting new goals, tracking your progress, and celebrating your wins. And when times get tough, don't forget to lean on your support system - your girlfriends, your family, and your own inner strength.

So go out there, *rock* your financial goals, and become the CEO of your own life. We believe in you, and we can't wait to see you succeed. Keep shining, sis!

Chapter 4: Taking Stock of Your Finances: Assessing Your Current Financial Situation

Hey girlies! Are you ready to take control of your finances and *glow up* your bank account? Whether you're a broke college student or a *CEO* in the making, it's time to start assessing your current financial situation and making moves towards building your financial independence. In this chapter, we're going to *low-key* get real about your money and figure out where you stand.

Now, I know talking about money can be intimidating, but trust me, it's *high-key* one of the most important things you can do for yourself. Being *woke* about your finances means being in control of your life and your future. And let's face it, being a *main character* in your own life story is way more fun than just going with the flow.

Let me tell you a little story. When I was in my early 20s, I was *extra* broke. I mean, I had negative money in my bank account and was living off of ramen noodles and tap water. It was not a good look. But, I realized that if I wanted to live the life I dreamed of, I needed to take control of my finances. So, I started assessing my current financial situation, and it was not pretty. I had no savings, no plan for paying off my student loans, and was spending money on things I didn't really need.

But, once I took the time to really look at my finances and make a plan, things started to turn around. I started saving money, paying off my debts, and even started investing. Now, I'm not saying I'm a financial expert, but I am saying that taking control of my finances changed my life for the better.

So, sis, if I can do it, you can do it too. It's time to start assessing your current financial situation and making moves towards building your financial independence. In this chapter, we'll talk about things like creating a budget, understanding your debt, and setting financial goals. Trust me, it's going to *slap* and you'll feel like a total *boss* once you're in control of your finances. Let's do this!

So, let's dive in. Here are some steps you can take to assess your financial health:

1. **Review your income.** Take a look at your income sources and how much money you're bringing in each month. Do you have a steady, reliable income, or are you relying on side hustles and gig work? Are there opportunities to increase your income, like negotiating a raise or starting a new job?

2. **Track your expenses.** It's important to know where your money is going each month. Track your expenses for a month or two to get a better understanding of your spending habits. Identify areas where you can cut back on expenses, like eating out less or cancelling subscriptions you don't use.

3. **Evaluate your debt.** Take a look at your debts, including credit card debt, student loans, and any other loans you have. How much debt do you have, and what are the interest rates and monthly payments? Are there any opportunities to refinance or consolidate your debt to save money on interest?

4. **Assess your savings.** How much money do you have saved, and where is it being held? Do you have an emergency fund in case of unexpected expenses? Are you saving for your long-term goals, like retirement or a down payment on a house?

5. **Check your credit score.** Your credit score can impact your ability to get loans and credit, so it's important to know where you stand. Check your credit score and take steps to improve it if necessary.

Once you've taken stock of your finances, you can start to identify areas where you need to improve and make a plan to reach your goals. Here are some tips to help you get started:

- **Create a budget.** Use the information you gathered about your income and expenses to create a budget that works for you. Identify areas where you can cut back on expenses and allocate more money towards your savings and debt repayment.

- **Make a debt repayment plan.** If you have debt, create a plan to pay it off as quickly as possible. Focus on paying off high-interest debt first, and consider options like refinancing or consolidating your debt to save money on interest.
- **Increase your savings.** Make sure you're saving enough to meet your long-term goals, like retirement and a down payment on a house. Consider opening a high-yield savings account or investing in a retirement account to maximize your savings.
- **Monitor your progress.** Use a spreadsheet or a budgeting app to track your progress towards your goals. Celebrate your successes and make adjustments as needed.

Remember, improving your financial health takes time and effort. But by taking these steps to assess your financial situation and make a plan to reach your goals, you're setting yourself up for long-term success.

BOSSING INVESTMENTS: A SMART GIRL'S GUIDE TO BUILDING WEALTH

Alright girlfriends, that's a wrap on Chapter 4! You've made it through the tough stuff and now you're well on your way to financial freedom. Assessing your current financial situation is the first step towards taking control of your finances, and I'm so proud of you for taking that step.

Remember, building financial independence is a journey, not a destination. It takes time and effort, but it's so worth it in the end. You deserve to live the life you dream of, and being in control of your finances is a key part of making that happen.

So keep up the good work, stay focused on your goals, and don't forget to celebrate your wins along the way. You are a *boss* and you've got this. See you in the next chapter, girlies!

Chapter 5: Investing 101: A Beginner's Guide to the Stock Market

Girlies, have you ever felt overwhelmed when it comes to the world of investing? Do terms like "stocks" and "dividends" make your head spin? Well, girlfriend, you are not alone. Many of us have been conditioned to believe that investing is something only *bigwigs* and *Wall Street CEOs* can do, but the truth is, anyone can invest and build financial independence.

Periodt.

Investing is like a *glow up* for your bank account, and it's time for us to get *woke* and take control of our financial futures. In this chapter, we will go over the basics of the stock market and how you can start investing with just a few *bucks*.

But before we dive into the nitty-gritty, let me tell you a personal story. When I was in college, I worked part-time at a coffee shop, and I had this *extra* annoying customer who would always come in and talk about his investments. At the time, I didn't care much for it, but fast forward a few years, and that customer ended up being a millionaire. *Wow.*

The point is, investing is not just for the rich or the *main characters* in movies. It's for everyone, including you, sis.

Now, let's sip some tea and talk about the basics. The stock market is essentially a place where companies sell pieces of their ownership to the public in the form of stocks. When you buy a stock, you own a small piece of that company, and if the company does well, the value of your stock goes up, and you make a profit.

But investing also comes with risks. The value of stocks can fluctuate, and there's always a chance that you could lose money. That's why it's important to do your research and invest in companies that you believe in and have a good track record.

Investing can be a scary thing, but it can also be a *high-key* exciting way to build your wealth and achieve financial freedom. So let's get our CEO mindset on and start investing.

BOSSING INVESTMENTS: A SMART GIRL'S GUIDE TO BUILDING WEALTH

Investing is all about putting your money to work for you. When you invest, you're buying ownership in a company, and as the company grows and becomes more profitable, the value of your investment increases. There are many different types of investments, but for the purposes of this chapter, we'll focus on the stock market.

The stock market is where companies go to raise money by selling shares of their ownership. When you buy a share of a company's stock, you become a part-owner of the company. The value of your investment is tied to the performance of the company.

So, how do you get started with investing in the stock market? Here are some key steps:

1. **Research different types of investments.** There are many different types of investments, from stocks to bonds to mutual funds. Do your research and identify which types of investments align with your financial goals and risk tolerance.

2. **Open an investment account.** In order to invest in the stock market, you'll need to open an investment account. You can do this through a brokerage firm, which is a company that facilitates buying and selling of stocks and other investments.

3. **Choose stocks to invest in.** Once you have an investment account, you can start buying stocks. Do your research and identify companies that you believe will perform well over time. Consider factors like the company's financials, leadership, and industry trends.

4. **Diversify your investments.** It's important to diversify your investments, which means spreading your money across multiple companies and industries. This can help reduce your overall risk and protect your portfolio from downturns in specific sectors.

5. **Monitor your investments.** The stock market can be volatile, so it's important to keep an eye on your investments and

make adjustments as needed. Consider setting up automatic investments and using a tool like a stock tracker app to monitor your portfolio.

Remember, investing in the stock market involves risk. The value of your investments can fluctuate and you may not get back your initial investment. That being said, investing can also be a great way to grow your wealth over time.

If you're new to investing, consider working with a financial advisor or doing more research to ensure you're making informed investment decisions. With a little bit of knowledge and a lot of patience, investing in the stock market can be a smart move for building wealth over the long term.

BOSSING INVESTMENTS: A SMART GIRL'S GUIDE TO BUILDING WEALTH

Well, girlfriends, we did it! We made it through Investing 101, and now you have the tools to start building your financial independence. Remember, investing is not just for the *bigwigs* and Wall Street CEOs, it's for everyone, including you.

Don't be afraid to do your research, take calculated risks, and invest in companies that you believe in. And if you ever feel lost or confused, don't hesitate to reach out to a financial advisor or do some more research.

Building wealth takes time, patience, and dedication, but with a little effort and the right mindset, you can achieve financial freedom and live the life you've always dreamed of.

So go out there and invest, girliezzz!

Chapter 6: Investing for the Long Term: Building a Diversified Portfolio

Girlies, it's time to talk about *investing*. I know, I know, it sounds like a snooze-fest. But trust me, it's actually *super important* for our financial *glow up*.

Think about it: we work hard for our money, right? So why not make our money work hard for us? That's where investing comes in.

Now, I'm not talking about throwing all your cash into some sketchy get-rich-quick scheme. No, no, no. We're talking about building a *diversified portfolio*. And if you're scratching your head wondering what the heck that even means, don't worry. I gotchu, fam.

Basically, a diversified portfolio is a fancy way of saying you're spreading your investments across a bunch of different *things*. Like stocks, bonds, mutual funds, real estate, and more. The idea is that if one thing *slaps* and another thing *flops*, you're not putting all your eggs in one basket.

But why should we care about a diversified portfolio? Well, for starters, it can *reduce risk*. If you've got all your money in one stock and that stock tanks, you're screwed. But if you've got your money spread out, you're *low-key* protected.

Plus, a diversified portfolio can *increase returns* over the long term. And that's really what we're after, right? We want our money to grow so we can live our best lives.

Now, I know this all sounds a little intimidating. But don't worry, sis. We're gonna walk through it step-by-step. And by the end of this chapter, you're gonna be a *CEO* of your own investments. Periodt.

So let's sip some tea, get *woke* about investing, and become the *main character* of our financial futures.

Are you with me, girlfriends? Let's do this.

So, how do you build a diversified portfolio? Here are some key steps:

- **Identify your financial goals.** Before you start investing, it's important to identify your financial goals. Are you saving for retirement, a down payment on a house, or another big expense? Understanding your goals can help you determine how much risk you're willing to take on.
- **Determine your risk tolerance.** Your risk tolerance is the amount of risk you're willing to take on in your investments. Are you comfortable with higher-risk investments that have the potential for greater returns, or do you prefer lower-risk investments with more predictable returns?
- **Allocate your investments.** Once you've identified your financial goals and risk tolerance, you can start allocating your investments. Consider spreading your investments across multiple asset classes, such as stocks, bonds, and cash. Within each asset class, consider diversifying your investments by sector and company.
- **Monitor your portfolio.** It's important to regularly review your portfolio and make adjustments as needed. Consider rebalancing your investments periodically to ensure that your portfolio remains aligned with your financial goals and risk tolerance.

Remember, diversification doesn't guarantee profits or protect against losses. It's important to work with a financial advisor or do your research to ensure that your investments are aligned with your goals and risk tolerance.

Investing for the long term requires patience and discipline. By building a diversified portfolio and monitoring your investments over time, you can set yourself up for long-term success.

And there you have it, fam! Investing for the long-term doesn't have to be scary. In fact, it can be downright empowering. By building a diversified portfolio, we're taking control of our finances and making our money work harder for us.

So let's promise each other that we won't shy away from investing anymore. Let's get *extra* and make our money work as hard as we do.

Remember, a diversified portfolio can *reduce risk* and *increase returns* over the long term. And that's a *slap* in the face to anyone who ever doubted us.

So go forth, my fellow CEOs. Build that diversified portfolio, and watch your financial future *glow up*.

Chapter 7: How to Evaluate Stocks: Understanding Key Metrics and Ratios

Welcome back, boss ladies! In Chapter 5, we talked about the basics of investing in the stock market, and in Chapter 6, we discussed building a diversified portfolio for the long term.

Now, it's time to get *woke* about your money. You're the *main character* of your own life, and that means taking control of your finances. You might be feeling like a *hot mess* when it comes to stocks, but don't worry, sis, we've got you covered. In this chapter, we're going to teach you how to evaluate stocks like a *CEO*, so you can build your own financial *empire*.

First things first, let's talk about why stocks are such a big deal. Investing in stocks can be a *slap* in the face for anyone who's used to just saving their money in a bank account. Stocks have the potential to grow your money much faster than a traditional savings account. But, before you start throwing all your cash at the stock market, you need to know how to evaluate stocks to make sure you're making smart choices.

In this chapter, we're going to go over some key metrics and ratios that will help you understand the value of a company and its stock. You'll learn about things like price-to-earnings ratios, market capitalization, and dividend yields. Don't worry, we'll explain what all of those mean in plain English, so you can make sense of it all.

We'll talk about how a company's management team can impact its stock value, and why it's important to do your own research instead of just following the crowd.

By the end of this chapter, you'll be ready to evaluate stocks like a pro. You'll know how to spot a good investment opportunity and how to steer clear of *extra* risk. So, get ready to *glow up* your financial knowledge and take control of your financial future. High-key, it's going to be *lit*.

BOSSING INVESTMENTS: A SMART GIRL'S GUIDE TO BUILDING WEALTH

Investing in stocks can be overwhelming and confusing, especially for those who are new to the game. But evaluating stocks is essential to making informed investment decisions that can help you build wealth over time. In this chapter, we'll break down some key metrics and ratios that can help you evaluate stocks like a boss.

- **Price-to-Earnings (P/E) Ratio:** The P/E ratio is a valuation ratio that compares a company's stock price to its earnings per share (EPS). It's one of the most widely used metrics for evaluating stocks. A higher P/E ratio can indicate that a company is overvalued, while a lower P/E ratio can indicate that a company is undervalued. However, it's important to keep in mind that a high P/E ratio doesn't always mean a company is overvalued, and a low P/E ratio doesn't always mean a company is undervalued.
  For example, let's say Company A has a P/E ratio of 25, while Company B has a P/E ratio of 10. At first glance, it might seem like Company B is the better investment since it has a lower P/E ratio. However, it's important to look at other factors as well, such as the industry in which the companies operate, their financials, and their leadership.
- **Price-to-Sales (P/S) Ratio:** The P/S ratio compares a company's stock price to its revenue per share. This can be a useful metric for evaluating companies that may not have consistent earnings but generate consistent revenue. Like the P/E ratio, a higher P/S ratio can indicate that a company is overvalued, while a lower P/S ratio can indicate that a company is undervalued.
  For example, let's say Company C has a P/S ratio of 5, while Company D has a P/S ratio of 1.5. In this case, Company D may be the better investment since it has a lower P/S ratio. However, it's important to look at other factors as well to

make an informed decision.

- **Price-to-Book (P/B) Ratio:** The P/B ratio compares a company's stock price to its book value per share. This can be a useful metric for evaluating companies that have a lot of assets or tangible value. A lower P/B ratio can indicate that a company is undervalued, while a higher P/B ratio can indicate that a company is overvalued.

- **Debt-to-Equity (D/E) Ratio:** The D/E ratio compares a company's debt to its equity. A higher D/E ratio can indicate that a company is taking on too much debt and may be at risk for financial instability. On the other hand, a lower D/E ratio can indicate that a company is financially stable and less likely to face financial difficulties.

- **Return on Equity (ROE):** The ROE is a measure of how much profit a company generates for each dollar of shareholder equity. A higher ROE can indicate that a company is efficient and generating strong returns for its shareholders.

- **Dividend Yield:** The dividend yield is the amount of dividends paid by a company per share, expressed as a percentage of the stock price. This can be a useful metric for evaluating companies that pay regular dividends to their shareholders.

While these metrics and ratios can be helpful in evaluating stocks, it's important to note that they shouldn't be the only factor you consider. It's important to also look at the company's financials, leadership, industry trends, and other relevant factors.

In addition to these metrics, there are many other factors to consider when evaluating stocks, such as the company's growth potential, competitive landscape, and market trends. It can be overwhelming, but with time and practice, you can become a savvy stock evaluator.

One way to practice evaluating stocks is to use stock screening tools, which can help you filter stocks based on specific criteria, such as P/E ratio, market cap, or dividend yield. You can also read up on industry trends and company news to stay informed about the companies you're considering investing in.

Remember, investing in the stock market involves risk, and it's important to do your due diligence and make informed decisions based on your individual financial situation and goals. Don't be afraid to seek out professional advice or guidance if you're unsure about a particular investment.

By understanding key metrics and ratios and taking the time to evaluate stocks, you can make informed investment decisions that can help you build wealth and achieve financial independence.

Now, let's put your knowledge to the test with a quiz. Grab a pen and paper and answer the following questions:

- What is the P/E ratio, and how can it be used to evaluate stocks?
- What is the P/S ratio, and how can it be used to evaluate stocks?
- What is the P/B ratio, and how can it be used to evaluate stocks?
- What is the D/E ratio, and how can it be used to evaluate stocks?
- What is the ROE, and how can it be used to evaluate stocks?
- What is the dividend yield, and how can it be used to evaluate stocks?

Once you've completed the quiz, take a look at your answers and assess your knowledge. If you struggled with any of the questions, don't worry - it takes time and practice to become a confident stock evaluator.

In conclusion, evaluating stocks can be an intimidating task, but it's an important step in making informed investment decisions. By understanding key metrics and ratios like the P/E ratio, P/S ratio, P/B ratio, D/E ratio, ROE, and dividend yield, you can make more informed decisions about the stocks you want to invest in. However, keep in mind that these metrics should not be the only factor you consider. It's also essential to research the company's financials, leadership, industry trends, and other relevant factors.

As a boss lady, it's important to remember that investing involves risk, and it's important to do your due diligence and make informed decisions based on your individual financial situation and goals. Don't be afraid to seek out professional advice or guidance if you're unsure about a particular investment.

So, girlies, put your knowledge to the test and assess your understanding of these key metrics and ratios with the quiz provided. Keep learning and growing your financial knowledge, and don't be afraid to take risks and invest in your financial glow up. You're a boss lady who can evaluate stocks like a CEO, periodt.

Chapter 8:
Understanding Risk and Return: How to Manage Risk in Your Portfolio

Hey there girlies, it's your main character coming at you with some financial wisdom. Are you ready to glow up your finances? Today, we're talking about managing risk in your portfolio.

Let's be real, investing can be scary. There are so many unknowns and it's easy to feel like you're throwing your money into a black hole. But, taking risks is a part of life and investing is no different.

First, let's talk about risk. Risk is the possibility that your investment won't turn out the way you hoped. It's like going on a blind date - you could hit it off or it could be a total disaster. But, just like dating, you can manage risk to increase your chances of success.

That's where return comes in. Return is the money you make on your investment. It's like when you order a delicious meal and it *slaps* - you're getting something good out of it.

But, as we all know, nothing in life comes for free. The higher the return, the higher the risk. You have to be *woke* to the tradeoff between risk and return.

So, how do you manage risk in your portfolio? Diversification is key. Don't put all your eggs in one basket, sis. Spread your investments across different assets and industries. This way, if one investment goes south, it won't tank your whole portfolio.

And, don't forget to check your emotions at the door. It's easy to get swept up in the hype of a high-key investment opportunity, but remember to do your research and make informed decisions.

At the end of the day, we're all CEOs of our own finances. Take control and manage your risk to increase your chances of financial success. Let's get extra with our finances, girlfriend.

Investing in the stock market involves risk, and it's important to understand the relationship between risk and return. In general, the higher the potential return, the higher the risk. Conversely, the lower the risk, the lower the potential return. This is known as the risk-return tradeoff.

While it's natural to want high returns on our investments, it's important to remember that taking on too much risk can lead to significant losses. That's why it's crucial to manage risk in your investment portfolio.

So, how can you manage risk in your portfolio? Let's dive in.

Diversification

One of the most effective ways to manage risk in your portfolio is through diversification. Diversification involves investing in a variety of assets, such as stocks, bonds, and mutual funds, across different sectors and industries. By spreading your investments across different types of assets, you can reduce the impact of any one investment on your overall portfolio.

For example, if you only invest in one stock and that stock experiences a significant drop in value, your entire portfolio will be impacted. However, if you invest in multiple stocks across different sectors and industries, the impact of any one stock's performance will be less significant.

Asset Allocation

Asset allocation involves dividing your portfolio among different asset classes, such as stocks, bonds, and cash. The right mix of asset classes will depend on your individual financial situation and goals.

Generally, stocks offer higher potential returns but also higher risk, while bonds offer lower potential returns but lower risk. Cash provides stability and liquidity but may not keep up with inflation.

It's important to find the right balance between risk and return and to regularly reevaluate your asset allocation to ensure it aligns with your goals.

Risk Tolerance

Your risk tolerance is your ability to handle the ups and downs of the stock market. It's important to be honest with yourself about your risk tolerance and to only invest in assets that align with it.

If you're uncomfortable with high-risk investments, consider investing in more stable assets, such as bonds or mutual funds. If you're comfortable with higher risk, you may consider investing in individual stocks or other high-growth assets.

Investment Horizon

Your investment horizon is the length of time you plan to hold your investments. Generally, the longer your investment horizon, the more risk you can take on.

If you have a longer investment horizon, you may consider investing in higher-risk assets, such as stocks, which have the potential for higher returns over the long term. If your investment horizon is shorter, you may want to consider more stable assets, such as bonds.

Managing risk in your investment portfolio is crucial to building long-term wealth and achieving financial independence. By diversifying your investments, allocating your assets wisely, being honest about your risk tolerance, and considering your investment horizon, you can create a balanced and successful investment portfolio.

Now, let's put your knowledge to the test with a quiz. Grab a pen and paper and answer the following questions:

- What is the risk-return tradeoff, and how does it apply to investing?

- What is diversification, and how can it help manage risk in your portfolio?
- What is asset allocation, and how can it help manage risk in your portfolio?
- What is risk tolerance, and why is it important to consider when managing your portfolio?
- What is investment horizon, and how can it impact your investment decisions?

One of the biggest reasons to manage risk in your portfolio is to minimize losses. By keeping your portfolio diversified and managing your risk, you can reduce the chances of incurring large losses that could potentially wipe out your savings.

Another important aspect of managing risk is understanding your own risk tolerance. Every individual has a different tolerance for risk, and it's important to invest in a way that aligns with your personal comfort level. If you're more risk-averse, you may want to consider investing in safer, more conservative assets such as bonds, while if you're comfortable with taking on more risk, you may want to explore more high-risk, high-reward investments like stocks.

To help manage your risk, it's also important to regularly review and rebalance your portfolio. Over time, certain assets may perform better than others, causing your portfolio to become unbalanced. By rebalancing and readjusting your investments as needed, you can help maintain your desired level of risk and keep your portfolio on track.

In addition, it's important to do your due diligence when it comes to researching and selecting investments. Take the time to thoroughly research any potential investments, and be wary of any promises of guaranteed returns or "get-rich-quick" schemes. Remember that investing always comes with a level of risk, and it's important to be realistic about your expectations and the potential outcomes.

Managing risk can seem intimidating, but with a little education and attention, it's possible to build a portfolio that meets your goals while minimizing your exposure to risk. By staying disciplined and consistent in your approach, you can build a portfolio that not only generates returns, but also helps protect your hard-earned savings.

Remember: managing risk is not about avoiding it altogether, but about finding the right balance of risk and reward that aligns with your personal goals and values.

One of the best ways to manage risk in your portfolio is to diversify your investments. This means investing in a variety of different assets, such as stocks, bonds, real estate, and commodities, in order to spread your risk across multiple sectors and industries. By diversifying your portfolio, you can help protect your investments from the ups and downs of any one particular market or industry.

It's also important to keep an eye on external factors that could impact your portfolio's performance, such as changes in interest rates, inflation, and geopolitical events. While you can't control these external factors, you can prepare for them by building a portfolio that's able to weather a variety of market conditions.

Another key factor in managing risk is maintaining a long-term perspective. Investing is a marathon, not a sprint, and it's important to stay patient and focused on your long-term goals. While short-term fluctuations in the market can be unnerving, it's important to remember that over the long term, the stock market has historically delivered strong returns.

When it comes to managing risk, there is no one-size-fits-all solution. The right approach for you will depend on your personal financial goals, risk tolerance, and investment timeline. However, by staying disciplined, diversifying your investments, and keeping a long-term perspective, you can help manage your risk and build a portfolio that supports your financial future.

BOSSING INVESTMENTS: A SMART GIRL'S GUIDE TO BUILDING WEALTH

There are a number of tools and strategies available to help you manage risk in your portfolio. One common approach is to use asset allocation, which involves dividing your investments among different asset classes based on your risk tolerance and investment goals. For example, you may decide to allocate a certain percentage of your portfolio to stocks, bonds, and other asset classes based on your individual needs.

Another way to manage risk is through the use of stop-loss orders, which are designed to limit your losses by automatically selling an investment if it falls below a certain price. This can be a helpful way to protect against sudden drops in the market, but it's important to remember that stop-loss orders are not foolproof and may not always be able to prevent losses.

When it comes to managing risk in your portfolio, it's also important to be mindful of your own behavior. Emotional reactions to market fluctuations, such as panic selling or chasing returns, can lead to poor investment decisions and ultimately harm your portfolio's performance. By staying disciplined and avoiding knee-jerk reactions, you can help ensure that your investment decisions are grounded in logic and reason rather than emotion.

Ultimately, managing risk is about finding the right balance between risk and reward that's appropriate for your individual needs and goals. By staying informed, diversifying your investments, and staying disciplined, you can help protect your investments and achieve long-term financial success.

Girlies, we made it to the end of this chapter on managing risk in your investment portfolio! *Periodt.* Investing in the stock market can be intimidating, but by understanding the relationship between risk and return, and by implementing strategies to manage risk, you can build a secure financial future for yourself.

The risk-return tradeoff is a key concept in investing, and it's important to find the right balance of risk and return that aligns with your personal goals and values. Diversification, asset allocation, risk tolerance, and investment horizon are all important factors to consider when building a balanced and successful investment portfolio.

Remember, it's crucial to regularly review and rebalance your portfolio to ensure that it aligns with your goals and risk tolerance. And while it's natural to want high returns on your investments, it's important to be realistic about the potential risks and to avoid "get-rich-quick" schemes that promise unrealistic returns.

Managing risk in your portfolio is not about avoiding risk altogether, but about finding the right balance of risk and reward that aligns with your individual goals and values. By staying disciplined, diversifying your investments, and keeping a long-term perspective, you can help manage your risk and build a portfolio that supports your financial future.

Now it's time to put your knowledge into action. Use the quiz at the end of this chapter to test your understanding of key concepts, and consider revisiting some of the tips and strategies we discussed throughout the chapter. By staying informed and taking a proactive approach to managing risk in your portfolio, you can build a secure financial future for yourself.

And remember, fam, investing is a journey, not a destination. It takes time, discipline, and patience to build wealth and achieve financial independence. But with the right mindset and strategies, you can take control of your finances and build a bright financial future for yourself. *You got this, sis. You're the CEO of your financial life.*

Chapter 9: Creating a Budget: Managing Your Money Day to Day

Alright, girlies, it's time to get down to the nitty-gritty of managing your money like a CEO. We're talking about creating a budget, and let me tell you, it's not as boring as it sounds. In fact, creating a budget can be the key to your financial *glow up*.

I know, I know, budgeting is not exactly the most glamorous thing in the world. It's like that extra green smoothie you force yourself to drink every morning for the sake of being healthy. But trust me, creating a budget is worth it, just like that green smoothie is worth it for the sake of your health.

When you have a budget, you have a clear plan for your money. You know how much you're making, how much you're spending, and where your money is going. This is crucial for achieving your financial goals, whether that's saving for a trip with your girlfriends or investing in your future.

Creating a budget can be a *high-key* empowering experience. It puts you in control of your money, and makes you feel like the main character of your financial story. You're no longer just letting your money slip through your fingers, you're taking charge and making intentional choices about how you use your money.

But, sis, let's keep it real. Budgeting can be tough, especially if you're used to spending money on whatever you want, whenever you want. It's like when you finally realize that it's time to cut down on those daily *Starbucks runs* (yes, I went there). But don't worry, fam, I got you. In this chapter, we're going to talk about how to create a budget that works for you, and how to stick to it without feeling like you're missing out on all the fun.

So, grab a cup of tea, get comfy, and let's dive into the world of budgeting. It's time to take control of your money and get *woke* about your finances. Periodt.

Why Budgeting is Important

Budgeting is important for several reasons:

- **Helps You Reach Your Financial Goals** - A budget can help you reach your financial goals by showing you where your money is going and helping you prioritize your spending. Whether you want to save for a down payment on a house, pay off debt, or take a dream vacation, a budget can help you get there.
- **Keeps You on Track** - A budget helps you stay on track with your spending, so you don't overspend and end up in debt. It can also help you avoid impulse purchases and stick to your financial goals.
- **Provides a Safety Net** - A budget can provide a safety net by helping you set aside money for unexpected expenses, like car repairs or medical bills. By creating an emergency fund, you can avoid going into debt when unexpected expenses arise.

Creating a Budget

Creating a budget can seem overwhelming, but it's easier than you think. Here's a step-by-step guide to creating your own budget:

- **Determine Your Income** - The first step in creating a budget is to determine your income. This includes any money you receive, including your salary, side hustles, and investments.
- **Calculate Your Essential Expenses** - Next, calculate your essential expenses. These are expenses that you need to pay in order to live, like rent or mortgage payments, utilities, food, and transportation. Make sure to include all your monthly bills, so you can accurately track your expenses.

- **Calculate Your Discretionary Expenses** - After you've calculated your essential expenses, it's time to calculate your discretionary expenses. These are expenses that are nice to have but not essential, like dining out or entertainment. Make sure to set aside money for these expenses, but keep in mind that they should not take up the majority of your budget.
- **Track Your Spending** - The next step is to track your spending. Keep track of all your expenses for a month, so you can see where your money is going. This will help you identify areas where you can cut back and areas where you may need to adjust your budget.
- **Adjust Your Budget** - After you've tracked your spending, it's time to adjust your budget. Look for areas where you can cut back, like dining out or entertainment expenses. You can also look for ways to save money on your essential expenses, like by shopping around for lower insurance rates or finding ways to save on your utilities.
- **Stick to Your Budget** - The final step is to stick to your budget. This can be challenging, especially at first, but it's important to stay committed to your financial goals. Make sure to check in on your budget regularly and adjust it as needed.

Calculate Your Net Income

The next step in creating a budget is to calculate your net income. Your net income is the money you have left over after taxes and other deductions are taken out of your paycheck. This is the money you have available to pay for your expenses and save for the future.

To calculate your net income, take your total income for the month and subtract all taxes and other deductions. This will give you your net income.

Categorize Your Expenses

The next step in creating a budget is to categorize your expenses. This means grouping your expenses into different categories, such as housing, transportation, food, entertainment, and so on. This will help you see where your money is going and where you can cut back if necessary.

To categorize your expenses, look at your bank statements and credit card statements for the past few months. Write down each expense and the amount you spent. Then, group these expenses into categories based on the type of expense.

Set Your Budget

Once you have calculated your net income and categorized your expenses, it's time to set your budget. This means deciding how much money you will spend in each category.

To set your budget, start with your essential expenses, such as rent or mortgage, utilities, food, and transportation. These expenses should be your first priority, and you should make sure you have enough money to cover them each month.

Next, look at your discretionary expenses, such as entertainment, dining out, and travel. These expenses are not essential, but they can make life more enjoyable. Decide how much you want to spend in each category and adjust as necessary to stay within your budget.

Monitor and Adjust Your Budget

Creating a budget is just the first step. To make it work, you need to monitor your spending and adjust your budget as needed. This means keeping track of your expenses throughout the month and making changes if you find that you are overspending in one category.

To monitor your budget, use a spreadsheet or budgeting app to track your expenses. Compare your actual spending to your budget each month, and make adjustments as needed.

In addition, be flexible with your budget. If unexpected expenses come up, you may need to adjust your budget to make room for them. Remember, a budget is a tool to help you manage your money, not a strict set of rules that you must follow no matter what.

Tips for Sticking to Your Budget Now that you have created your budget, the real challenge is sticking to it. Here are some tips to help you stay on track:

- **Use Cash**
  One of the easiest ways to stay within your budget is to use cash for discretionary expenses like dining out or entertainment. Withdraw the amount you have budgeted for these expenses in cash and use it instead of your debit or credit card. This way, you will be more aware of how much you are spending and will be less likely to overspend.
- **Automate Your Savings**
  One of the best ways to save money is to make it automatic. Set up a direct deposit from your paycheck into a savings account, so you don't have to think about it. This way, you will be less likely to spend the money you have designated for savings.
- **Use Budgeting Apps**
  Budgeting apps like Mint and You Need a Budget can help you stay on track with your spending. These apps connect to your bank and credit card accounts and automatically track your spending. They can also send you alerts when you are approaching your budget limits.

- **Track Your Progress**
  Make sure to track your progress throughout the month to see how you are doing. Use a spreadsheet or budgeting app to track your expenses and compare them to your budget. This will help you identify areas where you may need to adjust your budget.

- **Be Realistic**
  When setting your budget, make sure to be realistic about your expenses. Don't set a budget that is too restrictive or unrealistic, or you will be more likely to give up on it. Make sure to give yourself some wiggle room for unexpected expenses.

- **Celebrate Small Wins**
  Finally, make sure to celebrate small wins along the way. If you stick to your budget for a week or a month, reward yourself with something small, like a movie night at home or a favorite treat. This will help you stay motivated and committed to your financial goals.

Girlies, we made it to the end of the budgeting chapter! You may think budgeting is boring, but let me tell you, it's a total game-changer. Having a budget helps you reach your financial goals, keeps you on track with your spending, and provides a safety net for unexpected expenses. So, it's time to become a budgeting *CEO* and take control of your finances.

Creating a budget may seem intimidating, but it's easier than you think. The first step is to calculate your net income and categorize your expenses. This will help you see where your money is going and where you can cut back if necessary. Next, set your budget for each category and monitor your spending throughout the month.

To stick to your budget, try using cash for discretionary expenses, automate your savings, and use budgeting apps to track your spending. Remember to be realistic about your expenses, celebrate small wins along the way, and be flexible with your budget.

Managing your money like a *boss* takes discipline and dedication, but it's so worth it. Budgeting will help you achieve your financial goals and live the life you want. Don't let money stress you out - take control of your finances and glow up your financial situation.

Exercise:

Create a monthly budget for yourself. Use a spreadsheet or budgeting app to track your expenses, categorize them, and set a budget for each category. Monitor your spending throughout the month, and adjust your budget as needed. At the end of the month, review your progress and celebrate your wins. This exercise will help you create a budget that works for you and your financial goals.

Remember, girlies, you got this! Budgeting may not be the most *extra* thing to do, but it's essential for financial success. Stick to your budget, stay committed to your goals, and take control of your finances like the *main character* you are. Periodt.

Chapter 10: Managing Debt: Strategies for Paying Off Debt and Improving Your Credit Score

Hey girlies, let's talk about everyone's favorite topic... debt! *Sarcasm* We all know it's not fun to owe money to anyone, but it's a reality for many of us. Whether it's student loans, credit card debt, or a car loan, debt can be a major source of stress and anxiety.

But fear not, fam! It's never too late to start paying off your debt and improving your credit score. And trust me, the glow up you'll experience when you finally pay off that last debt will be *high-key* amazing.

In this chapter, we're going to dive into some practical strategies for managing debt and improving your credit score. We'll cover everything from creating a budget to paying off debt strategically, and we'll sip some tea on how to deal with debt collectors.

As a main character in your own life, it's important to take control of your finances and manage your debt wisely. When you're woke to the power of financial freedom, you'll see that being debt-free is the ultimate goal. Periodt.

Managing debt can be tough, but with the right strategies and mindset, you can take control of your finances and build a brighter financial future. Let's dive into this chapter and start making moves towards being debt-free, sis. You've got this!

Understanding Your Debt

The first step in managing your debt is to understand what you owe. Make a list of all your debts, including the creditor, the balance owed, the interest rate, and the minimum payment. This will help you see the big picture and prioritize your debts.

Next, take a look at your credit score. Your credit score is a three-digit number that ranges from 300 to 850 and is used by lenders to assess your creditworthiness. The higher your credit score, the better your chances of being approved for loans and credit cards with favorable terms.

If your credit score is low, don't panic. There are steps you can take to improve your score, which we'll cover later in this chapter.

Strategies for Paying Off Debt

Once you understand your debt, it's time to create a plan for paying it off. Here are some strategies to consider:

- **Snowball Method** - This method involves paying off your debts from smallest to largest, regardless of interest rates. This can be a motivating way to see progress quickly.
- **Avalanche Method** - This method involves paying off your debts with the highest interest rates first, which can save you money in the long run.
- **Debt Consolidation** - This involves taking out a new loan to pay off all your debts, leaving you with one monthly payment at a lower interest rate. This can be a good option if you have high-interest credit card debt.
- **Debt Settlement** - This involves negotiating with your creditors to settle your debts for less than what you owe. This should be a last resort, as it can have a negative impact on

your credit score.

Whichever method you choose, make sure to continue making the minimum payments on all your debts to avoid late fees and damage to your credit score.

Improving Your Credit Score

Improving your credit score can take time, but there are steps you can take to speed up the process. Here are some tips to consider:

- **Pay on Time** - Your payment history is the most important factor in your credit score, so make sure to pay all your bills on time.
- **Keep Your Credit Utilization Low** - Your credit utilization is the amount of credit you're using compared to your credit limit. Keep this below 30% to avoid damaging your credit score.
- **Don't Close Old Credit Accounts** - The length of your credit history is another important factor in your credit score. Keep your old credit accounts open to maintain a long credit history.
- **Monitor Your Credit Report** - Check your credit report regularly for errors or fraudulent activity. You can get a free copy of your credit report once a year from each of the three major credit bureaus.
- **Consider a Secured Credit Card** - If you're struggling to get approved for a traditional credit card, consider a secured credit card, which requires a cash deposit as collateral.

In addition to these tips, it's important to be patient and persistent. Improving your credit score takes time, but it's worth the effort.

Exercise: Creating a Debt Repayment Plan

Now that you understand your debt and have strategies for paying it off, it's time to create a debt repayment plan. Use the following steps to create your plan:

1. Make a list of all your debts, including the creditor, balance owed, interest rate, and minimum monthly payment.
2. Prioritize your debts by interest rate, starting with the debt with the highest interest rate.
3. Determine how much extra money you can put towards debt repayment each month. This could come from cutting back on discretionary spending or increasing your income with a side hustle.
4. Use the debt snowball or debt avalanche method to pay off your debts. With the debt snowball method, you pay off your debts from smallest to largest, regardless of interest rate. With the debt avalanche method, you pay off your debts from highest to lowest interest rate. Choose the method that works best for you.
5. Once you've paid off one debt, roll the money you were paying towards it into paying off the next debt on your list. This will help you pay off your debts faster and more efficiently.
6. Make sure to make at least the minimum payments on all your debts to avoid late fees and penalties.
7. Monitor your progress and adjust your plan as necessary. Celebrate your wins along the way to stay motivated.

Congratulations, girlfriends! You've made it to the end of our chapter on managing debt, and I hope you're feeling empowered and ready to take control of your finances.

Remember, being in debt doesn't make you a failure, but it's important to take action and manage your debt wisely. By creating a budget, paying off high-interest debt first, negotiating with debt collectors, and improving your credit score, you'll be on the path to financial freedom.

Here are some key takeaways to keep in mind:

- *Be intentional with your money.* Don't let your money control you, control your money. Be intentional with how you spend and save your money, and always look for ways to reduce your debt.
- *Don't be afraid to ask for help.* Managing debt can be overwhelming, but you don't have to do it alone. Reach out to a financial advisor or a credit counseling agency for help and guidance.
- *Stay focused on your goals.* Paying off debt and improving your credit score takes time and effort. Stay focused on your goals, and don't let setbacks discourage you. Celebrate your wins along the way and keep moving forward.

Always remember, sis, that you're the queen of your own life. So don't let debt hold you back from achieving your financial goals. Take charge of your finances and manage your debt like the boss that you are. With the right mindset and strategies, you can conquer your debt and build a brighter financial future. Keep pushing forward, because you've got this!

Chapter 11: Saving for the Future: Retirement Planning and Other Long-Term Goals

Hey girlies, are you ready to start planning for your future and securing your bag? Retirement planning and other long-term financial goals can feel overwhelming, but don't stress fam, we've got this.

Low-key, it's easy to get caught up in the moment and forget about planning for the future. But girl, trust me, the glow up is real when you start saving for retirement and other long-term goals. You'll be the main character of your life, and the periodt at the end of that sentence will be a big ol' pile of money.

So, sip your tea and let's dive into retirement planning and other long-term goals. It's time to get woke to the importance of saving and investing, and start taking action to secure your financial future. Whether you want to travel the world, start a business, or retire early, it all starts with taking small steps now.

In this chapter, we'll cover the following:

- *Why retirement planning and other long-term goals are important.* We'll go over the benefits of saving and investing for the future, and why it's important to start early.
- *How to set long-term financial goals.* We'll talk about how to set specific, measurable, achievable, relevant, and time-bound

(SMART) goals and create a plan to achieve them.

- *Ways to save and invest for the future.* We'll go over different options for saving and investing, including retirement accounts, stocks, and real estate.
- *Strategies for staying on track.* We'll cover ways to stay motivated and accountable for your financial goals, and how to adjust your plan as needed.

Investing in your future is like being the boss of your life. You're taking control of your finances and setting yourself up for success. So get ready to level up and let's start planning for your long-term goals. It's going to be a total game-changer for your financial future. Let's do this!

Retirement may seem far away, but it's important to start planning for it early. Here are some reasons why:

1. Time is on Your Side: The earlier you start saving for retirement, the more time your money has to grow. Starting early means you can take advantage of compound interest, which allows your money to grow faster over time.

2. Retirement May Be More Expensive Than You Think: Many people underestimate how much they will need for retirement. You may need to pay for healthcare costs, travel, and other expenses that you don't currently have.

3. Social Security May Not Be Enough: Social Security can provide some income in retirement, but it may not be enough to cover all your expenses. You may need to supplement your income with savings and investments.

4. It's Never Too Late to Start: Even if you haven't started saving for retirement, it's never too late to start. Every little bit helps, and you can still make a significant impact on your retirement savings by starting now.

Creating a Retirement Plan:

Creating a retirement plan can help you set and achieve your long-term goals. Here are some steps to get started:

1. Determine Your Retirement Goals: Think about what you want your retirement to look like. Do you want to travel? Volunteer? Spend time with family? Knowing your goals can help you determine how much you need to save.

2. Estimate Your Retirement Expenses: Estimate how much you will need to cover your retirement expenses. This includes things like housing, healthcare, food, and travel. Use online calculators or speak with a financial advisor to get a better

estimate.

3. Determine Your Retirement Income Sources: Determine where your retirement income will come from. This may include Social Security, pensions, and your savings and investments.

4. Calculate Your Retirement Gap: Calculate the difference between your retirement expenses and your expected retirement income. This will help you determine how much you need to save to cover the gap.

5. Start Saving: Start saving as early as possible. Aim to save at least 10-15% of your income for retirement. If you have access to a 401(k) or other retirement plan, take advantage of it. If not, consider opening an IRA or other retirement account.

Other Long-Term Goals:

Retirement isn't the only long-term goal you should be planning for. Here are some other goals to consider:

1. Saving for a Down Payment: If you plan to buy a house in the future, start saving for a down payment. This can help you secure a better interest rate and lower your monthly mortgage payment.

2. Saving for College: If you have children, start saving for their college education. Consider opening a 529 plan or other college savings account.

3. Building an Emergency Fund: Building an emergency fund can help you weather unexpected expenses, like car repairs or medical bills. Aim to save at least 3-6 months' worth of expenses in your emergency fund.

Exercise: Creating a Retirement Savings Plan

Use the following steps to create a retirement savings plan:

1. Determine your retirement goals.
2. Estimate your retirement expenses.
3. Determine your retirement income sources.
4. Calculate your retirement gap.
5. Start saving for retirement.

Well, well, well, girlfriend, you've made it to the end of our chat about saving for the future. And let me tell you, you're on your way to becoming the CEO of personal finance! By taking charge of your money and planning for the future, you're setting yourself up for a major glow up in the long run.

Chapter 12: Building Your Financial Team: How to Find a Financial Advisor You Can Trust

Hey girlies, welcome to Chapter 12 of "You Are a Badass at Making Money!" Are you ready to level up your financial game and build your dream life? If you are, then it's time to talk about building your financial team and finding a financial advisor you can trust.

I know, I know, talking to financial advisors can be scary and confusing. But trust me, having the right advisor on your team can help you *glow up* financially and achieve your goals. Think of them as your personal finance coach, here to guide you and support you on your journey to financial freedom.

In this chapter, we'll talk about how to find a financial advisor you can trust and build a solid financial team to help you achieve your goals. We'll cover everything from how to find an advisor, what to look for, and how to know if they're the right fit for you.

But before we dive in, let me share a personal story. I used to think that financial advisors were only for the *fam* with millions in the bank. But as I started to build my own wealth, I realized that having a trusted advisor on my team was essential. I wanted to make sure that I was making smart financial decisions and not just throwing my money away.

So, I did my research and found an advisor who was the right fit for me. We worked together to create a financial plan that aligned with my goals and values. And let me tell you, it was a game-changer. I felt more confident and empowered in my financial decisions, and I knew that I had a *main character* financial team supporting me every step of the way.

So, sis, if you're ready to take your financial game to the next level, it's time to find a financial advisor you can trust. Let's get started and *sip tea* on how to do just that. **Periodt!**

Why You Need a Financial Advisor

While it's possible to manage your finances on your own, a financial advisor can provide valuable guidance and expertise. Here are some reasons why you might want to consider working with a financial advisor:

1. **Expertise:** A financial advisor has the expertise and knowledge to help you make informed financial decisions. They can help you understand complex financial products and provide guidance on investments, taxes, and estate planning.

2. **Objectivity:** A financial advisor can provide an objective perspective on your finances. They can help you identify blind spots and biases that might be impacting your financial decisions.

3. **Accountability:** A financial advisor can hold you accountable for your financial goals. They can help you stay on track with your financial plan and make adjustments as needed.

4. **Time:** Managing your finances can be time-consuming. A financial advisor can help you save time by taking care of the details and providing you with a plan that fits your goals and lifestyle.

How to Find a Financial Advisor

Finding a financial advisor you can trust can be a challenge. Here are some tips to help you find the right advisor for your needs:

1. **Ask for Referrals:** Ask friends and family for referrals to financial advisors they've worked with and trust. Personal

recommendations can be a great way to find an advisor you feel comfortable with.

2. **Research Credentials**: Look for financial advisors who are certified and have the necessary credentials, such as Certified Financial Planner (CFP) or Chartered Financial Analyst (CFA). These designations indicate that the advisor has the education and experience needed to provide financial advice.

3. **Check for Disciplinary History**: Before working with a financial advisor, check for any disciplinary history or complaints. You can do this by researching the advisor's background with the Financial Industry Regulatory Authority (FINRA).

4. **Conduct Interviews**: Set up meetings with potential financial advisors to discuss your financial goals and get a sense of their approach. Ask about their experience, credentials, and fees. Make sure you feel comfortable with the advisor and their approach before making a decision.

5. **Review Fees**: Financial advisors typically charge fees based on a percentage of assets under management or an hourly rate. Make sure you understand the fees and how they will impact your finances before working with an advisor.

Working with Your Financial Advisor

Once you've found a financial advisor you can trust, it's important to establish a good working relationship. Here are some tips to help you get the most out of your financial advisor relationship:

1. **Communicate Openly**: Be open and honest with your financial advisor about your financial goals and concerns. This will help them create a plan that's tailored to your needs.

2. **Set Realistic Goals**: Work with your financial advisor to set realistic financial goals that align with your lifestyle and

values. This will help you stay motivated and on track.

3. **Review Your Plan**: Regularly review your financial plan with your advisor to ensure it's still aligned with your goals and needs. Make adjustments as needed to stay on track.

4. **Be Patient**: Building wealth takes time. Be patient and trust the process, even if you experience setbacks or obstacles along the way.

Exercise: Finding a Financial Advisor You Can Trust

Use the following questions to help you find a financial advisor you can trust:

1. *What financial goals do you want to achieve?*
2. *What qualifications and credentials do you want your financial advisor to have?*
3. *What fees are you comfortable paying for financial advice?*
4. *Are there any red flags or concerns you have when it comes to working with a financial advisor?*

Take the time to answer these questions and use them to guide your search for a financial advisor. Remember, finding the right advisor can take time, but it's worth the effort to find someone you trust to help you achieve your financial goals.

There you have it, girlfriends! Building a financial team that includes a trustworthy financial advisor can be a game-changer on your journey to financial independence. Just like a basketball team needs a great coach to win games, you need a financial advisor to guide you towards your financial goals.

Remember, finding the right financial advisor is crucial, so take your time and do your research. Look for an advisor who understands your values, listens to your needs, and communicates clearly. They should be there to support you, provide you with knowledge, and help you navigate the complex world of finance.

Don't forget that building a financial team is not just about finding an advisor, it's also about surrounding yourself with people who support and encourage you on your journey to financial freedom. This could include friends, family, or even a mentor who has experience in your field of work.

At the end of the day, your financial team is your support system. They're there to help you when times are tough, celebrate with you when you reach your goals, and keep you accountable along the way. So, don't be afraid to invest in yourself by building a strong financial team.

You're the G.O.A.T of your own financial journey, and with the right team on your side, you can achieve anything.

Chapter 13: Staying Motivated: How to Stay Focused on Your Goals

Hey there, my girlies! We all know that staying motivated is key to achieving our goals, especially when it comes to building financial independence. But let's be real, sometimes it's hard to stay focused and keep grinding towards our dreams. Life gets in the way, we get distracted, and our goals can start to feel out of reach.

That's why in this chapter, we're going to talk about how to stay motivated and stay focused on your financial goals. We'll share some tips and tricks to help you get back on track and stay the course, even when the going gets tough.

Staying motivated is all about mindset. It's about cultivating a positive and determined mindset that will keep you going no matter what. It's about being woke to your own potential and believing that you can achieve anything you set your mind to. It's about being the main character in your own story, and not letting anything stand in your way.

At the end of the day, sis, building financial independence is all about staying motivated and keeping your eye on the prize. It's about leveling up for yourself and your loved ones, and becoming the ultimate champ of your financial future. So let's get down to business, stay focused, and crush those financial goals like the boss babes we are!

Why Motivation Matters

Motivation is what drives us to take action and work towards our goals. Without motivation, it's easy to get stuck in a rut and lose sight of our objectives. When it comes to building wealth and achieving financial independence, motivation is key to staying on track.

Set Realistic Goals:

One of the most important things you can do to stay motivated is to set realistic financial goals. This means identifying goals that are achievable and relevant to your life. Goals that are too ambitious or unrealistic can lead to frustration and burnout, while goals that are too small or unimportant may not be motivating enough to keep you on track.

Here are some tips for setting realistic financial goals:

- Start by identifying your long-term financial goals, such as saving for retirement or buying a home.
- Break your long-term goals down into smaller, achievable milestones, such as saving a certain amount of money each month or paying off a credit card.
- Make sure your goals are relevant to your life and align with your values and priorities.
- Write down your goals and track your progress to stay motivated and focused.

Staying Motivated

Once you've set your financial goals, the next step is to find ways to stay motivated and focused on achieving them. Here are some strategies to help you stay on track:

1. Celebrate Small Wins: Building wealth takes time, and progress can be slow. It's important to celebrate the small wins along the way to stay motivated. Whether it's paying off a credit card or hitting a savings milestone, take time to acknowledge your progress and give yourself a pat on the back.

2. Find a Support System: Surround yourself with people who support and encourage your financial goals. This might mean finding a like-minded community online or in person, or working with a financial advisor or coach who can provide guidance and support.

3. Create a Vision Board: A vision board is a visual representation of your goals and dreams. Create a vision board that represents your financial goals, and place it somewhere you'll see it every day. This will help you stay motivated and focused on your objectives.

4. Stay Positive: Building wealth can be challenging, and setbacks are bound to happen. When things get tough, it's important to stay positive and keep a growth mindset. Focus on what you can control, and keep your eye on the big picture.

5. Keep Learning: Education is key to building financial literacy and staying motivated. Take advantage of free resources online, such as financial blogs and podcasts, and consider taking courses or attending workshops to expand your knowledge.

Exercise: Staying Motivated

Use the following questions to help you stay motivated and focused on your financial goals:

1. What are your long-term financial goals?

2. What are some achievable milestones you can set to work towards your goals?
3. Who can you turn to for support and encouragement?
4. How will you celebrate your progress along the way?
5. What can you do to stay positive and motivated, even when things get tough?

Motivation is the fuel that drives us towards our goals, and building financial independence is no exception. As we've discussed in this chapter, staying motivated is essential to achieving our financial goals, and it requires a combination of mindset, strategy, and support.

To stay motivated, it's important to set realistic financial goals, break them down into achievable milestones, and track your progress along the way. Celebrate the small wins, surround yourself with a supportive community, and keep a positive attitude even when things get tough.

Remember, building wealth is a journey, and setbacks are bound to happen. When they do, stay focused on the big picture, and keep learning and growing. Whether it's reading financial blogs, attending workshops, or working with a financial coach, education is key to building financial literacy and staying motivated.

So, my fellow boss babes, let's commit to staying motivated and focused on our financial goals. Let's be the CEOs of our financial future, and crush those financial goals like the extra queens we are. Don't let anything hold you back, because you have the power to achieve anything you set your mind to. Stay glowin' up and stay grinding, because the world is waiting for you to slay.

Chapter 14: Overcoming Roadblocks: Common Obstacles to Building Wealth and How to Overcome Them

Hey, my financially independent boss girlies!

I know the journey to building wealth can be exciting, but it can also be filled with roadblocks and obstacles. It's like a game of Mario Kart, where you have to dodge banana peels, avoid shells, and jump over hurdles to get to the finish line. But just like Mario Kart, with the right strategy and mindset, you can overcome any obstacle that comes your way.

In this chapter, we're going to talk about some common roadblocks to building wealth and how to overcome them. We'll cover everything from limiting beliefs and fears to practical challenges like debt and expenses. I'll share some personal stories and anecdotes to illustrate key concepts, and offer practical tips and actionable advice that you can use to overcome these roadblocks.

Remember, building wealth is not just about making money. It's about creating a mindset and a lifestyle that supports your financial goals. And that means overcoming the roadblocks that can get in your way. So, let's dive in and learn how to overcome those obstacles like the boss babes we are!

Key points to keep in mind as we go through this chapter:

- *Roadblocks are a normal part of the journey.* Don't be discouraged when you encounter roadblocks on your path to building wealth. It's all part of the process.
- *Your mindset is key.* Your beliefs and attitudes towards money can be roadblocks in and of themselves. It's important to identify and overcome limiting beliefs and fears that may be holding you back.
- *Practical challenges require practical solutions.* While mindset is important, it's also crucial to address practical challenges like debt and expenses with practical solutions.
- *You're not alone.* Remember, you're not the only one facing roadblocks on your financial journey. Many people, including successful entrepreneurs and investors, have faced and overcome similar challenges.

So buckle up, grab your controller, and get ready to power through those roadblocks like the badass young women we are. Let's do this!

Debt

Debt is one of the most common roadblocks to building wealth. It can be overwhelming and difficult to pay off, but it's important to tackle it head-on. Here are some tips for overcoming debt:

- Create a budget and stick to it. This will help you see where your money is going and where you can cut back to pay off debt.
- Prioritize high-interest debt first. Focus on paying off debt with the highest interest rates first to save money in the long run.
- Consider debt consolidation. Consolidating your debt can help you simplify your payments and potentially save money on interest.
- Avoid taking on new debt. Once you've paid off your debt, avoid taking on new debt unless it's absolutely necessary.

Unexpected Expenses

Unexpected expenses can be a major setback when it comes to building wealth. From car repairs to medical bills, these expenses can quickly drain your savings. Here are some tips for dealing with unexpected expenses:

- Build an emergency fund. Having an emergency fund can help you cover unexpected expenses without derailing your financial goals.
- Review your budget regularly. Make sure your budget includes a category for unexpected expenses so you're prepared when they arise.
- Consider insurance. Insurance can help protect you from

unexpected expenses, such as medical bills or car repairs.

Lack of Income

A lack of income can make it difficult to build wealth, but there are still steps you can take to improve your financial situation. Here are some tips for dealing with a lack of income:

- Explore new income streams. Consider taking on a part-time job or starting a side hustle to increase your income.
- Negotiate your salary. If you're employed full-time, consider negotiating your salary or asking for a raise.
- Cut back on expenses. Take a close look at your budget and see where you can cut back to free up some extra cash.

Lack of Knowledge

Lack of financial knowledge can be a major roadblock to building wealth. It can be overwhelming to try and navigate the complex world of finance on your own. Here are some tips for overcoming a lack of financial knowledge:

- Educate yourself. Read books, listen to podcasts, and take online courses to learn more about personal finance.
- Work with a financial advisor. A financial advisor can provide valuable guidance and help you navigate the world of finance.
- Seek out free resources. There are many free resources available online, such as personal finance blogs and forums.

Exercise: Overcoming Financial Roadblocks

Use the following questions to help you identify roadblocks to building wealth and come up with a plan for overcoming them:

- What is the biggest roadblock to building wealth in your life?
- What steps can you take to overcome this roadblock?
- What resources can you turn to for help and guidance?

We did it, girlies! We've covered some of the most common roadblocks to building wealth and how to overcome them. Debt, unexpected expenses, lack of income, and lack of financial knowledge can all seem like insurmountable obstacles, but with the right mindset and strategies, you can power through them and reach your financial goals.

Remember, building wealth is not a one-size-fits-all process. Everyone's journey is unique, and the roadblocks you face may be different from those of someone else. But no matter what challenges you encounter, there are always ways to overcome them.

The journey to financial independence can be a rollercoaster ride, full of ups and downs, twists and turns. But don't let the roadblocks discourage you. With the right mindset, strategies, and support, you can overcome any obstacle that comes your way and build the bright financial future you deserve.

So, keep pushing forward, girlies, and never lose sight of your financial goals. You've got this!

Chapter 15: The Power of Investing in Yourself: How to Leverage Your Skills and Talents to Build Wealth

Girlies, let's talk about investing in ourselves. I know, I know - the word "investing" can make you feel like you're about to read a boring textbook. But hear me out: investing in yourself is the *ultimate* glow up. Not only does it help you build wealth, but it also boosts your confidence, opens up new opportunities, and makes you feel like a total CEO.

Think about it - you're the main character of your own life story. And in order to have a plot that slaps, you need to invest in yourself. It's all about leveraging your skills and talents to create a future that's high-key amazing.

Now, I get it - investing money can be intimidating. But investing in *yourself*? That's something we can all get behind. Whether it's learning a new skill, taking a class, or networking with girlfriends who inspire you, investing in yourself is the ultimate power move.

And here's the best part: you don't need a ton of money to start investing in yourself. In fact, some of the best investments you can make are low-key free. It's all about recognizing your worth and taking the time to develop your skills and talents.

In this chapter, we're going to dive into the power of investing in yourself. We'll talk about why it's so important, how to identify your strengths, and practical tips for leveraging your talents to build financial independence. Trust me, by the end of this chapter, you'll be feeling extra woke and ready to take on the world.

So, let's get started sis.

Your future self will thank you.

Investing in yourself means taking the time, energy, and resources to develop your skills, talents, and knowledge. It's like planting seeds that will grow into a strong, healthy tree that will bear fruit for years to come. When you invest in yourself, you're building a solid foundation that will support you throughout your life, both financially and personally.

Here are some practical tips to help you invest in yourself and build wealth:

1. *Identify your skills and talents.* Take some time to think about what you're good at and what you enjoy doing. What skills and talents do you have that you can leverage to build wealth? Maybe you're a great writer, a talented artist, or a skilled negotiator. Whatever your strengths are, identify them and start thinking about how you can use them to your advantage.

2. *Find ways to develop your skills and talents.* Once you've identified your skills and talents, it's time to develop them further. There are many ways to do this, such as taking courses, attending workshops, practicing, or seeking mentorship. For example, if you're a writer, you could take a writing course or join a writing group to improve your skills. If you're an artist, you could attend an art workshop or work on your art every day to develop your talent.

3. *Network and build relationships.* Building relationships is key to success in any field. Connect with people who share your interests and goals, and seek mentorship and guidance from those who have more experience. Attend networking events, join groups or associations related to your field, and build your professional network. You never know who might be able to offer you a new opportunity or introduce you to someone who can help you grow.

4. *Take calculated risks.* Building wealth often requires taking risks. However, it's important to take calculated risks that are backed by solid research and planning. For example, if you're thinking of starting your own business, do your research and create a solid business plan before taking the leap. Don't be afraid to step out of your comfort zone, but make sure you're doing it in a smart and strategic way.

5. *Invest in education.* Education is one of the most powerful tools you can use to build wealth. Whether it's formal education or self-education, investing in learning will pay off in the long run. Take courses, read books, attend seminars, and learn from experts in your field. This will not only help you develop your skills and knowledge but also open up new opportunities for you.

6. *Stay disciplined and focused.* Building wealth requires discipline and focus. It's important to set clear goals and work towards them consistently. Develop good habits, such as saving regularly and avoiding unnecessary expenses. Keep track of your progress and celebrate your successes along the way.

Investing in yourself is not only about building wealth, but also about personal growth and fulfillment. When you invest in yourself, you're taking care of your own needs and building a better future for yourself. So, take the time to identify your skills and talents, develop them, build relationships, take calculated risks, invest in education, and stay disciplined and focused.

You've got this!

Exercise:

Create a list of your skills and talents. Next to each item, write down one thing you can do to develop it further. Make a plan to work on these skills and talents over the next few weeks or months, and set clear goals for what you want to achieve. For example, if one of your skills is public speaking, you could join a public speaking club, practice your speeches regularly, and set a goal to speak at a local event within the next six months.

Remember, investing in yourself is a continuous process. It's not something that happens overnight, but rather a journey that requires commitment and perseverance. Keep building your skills and talents, stay focused on your goals, and don't be afraid to take risks. Your future self will thank you for it.

In conclusion, investing in yourself is one of the most powerful things you can do to build wealth and achieve financial independence. By leveraging your skills and talents, building relationships, taking calculated risks, investing in education, and staying disciplined and focused, you can create a strong foundation that will support you throughout your life. So go ahead, my fellow badass young women, and invest in yourself like a boss!

Conclusion: Taking Action and Building a Bright Financial Future

GG! You've made it to the end of this book, and I hope you're feeling empowered and ready to take control of your finances. Remember, building financial independence is not about getting rich quick or winning the lottery. It's about taking small steps every day to create a bright financial future for yourself.

In this book, we've covered a lot of ground, from mindset shifts to practical strategies for building wealth. Here are some key takeaways to keep in mind as you move forward on your financial journey:

Believe in yourself and your ability to create wealth.

Your mindset is the foundation for your financial success. Believe that you have what it takes to create the life you want, and don't let limiting beliefs hold you back.

Take control of your finances.

Don't leave your financial future to chance. Take control of your money by creating a budget, tracking your expenses, and saving regularly.

Invest in your future.

Building wealth is a long-term game. Invest in your future by creating an emergency fund, saving for retirement, and building passive income streams.

Leverage your skills and talents.

You have unique skills and talents that can help you build wealth. Identify them, develop them, and use them to your advantage.

Build relationships and seek mentorship.

Building relationships is key to success in any field. Seek mentorship and guidance from those who have more experience, and build your professional network.

Stay disciplined and focused.

Building wealth requires discipline and focus. Set clear goals, develop good habits, and stay focused on your vision for the future.

Remember, building financial independence is a journey, not a destination. It's okay to make mistakes along the way, as long as you keep moving forward and learning from your experiences.

Exercise:

Create a financial vision board or list. This can be a physical or digital representation of what you want to achieve with your finances. It could include pictures, words, or symbols that represent your financial goals, such as a picture of your dream home, a symbol of financial freedom, or a quote that inspires you. Keep this vision board or list somewhere visible and refer to it regularly as a reminder of what you're working towards.

As you continue your financial journey, always remember that you're a total boss babe with the power to create the life you want. Keep taking small steps every day towards building a bright financial future and never be afraid to dream big. You've got this!

Also by Sophie Johnson

Bossing Up
Bossing Spreadsheets: A Girl's Guide to Data Analysis
Bossing Investments: A Smart Girl's Guide to Building Wealth

Standalone
The Social Media Manager's Handbook: Proven Strategies for
Building a Business Empire

www.ingramcontent.com/pod-product-compliance
Lightning Source LLC
Chambersburg PA
CBHW072132150726
48002CB00015B/2317